KNOTS OF CONFIDENCE:
PATKA AFFIRMATIONS

Rosey Kaur

Dedication

This book is a tribute to your unwavering spirit, resilience, and commitment to your faith and identity. In a world full of challenges and uncertainties, stand tall while wearing your Patka. It is a symbol of your connection to the Sikh faith and its values.

May these affirmations be a guiding light on your journey, providing strength, confidence, and a profound sense of self-worth. With each page, may you find empowerment and inspiration to embrace your unique identity and face the world with courage.

With much love,

Rosey Kaur

Wearing the Patka empowers my
inner strength.

I feel confident and secure when I wear my Patka.

The Patka enhances my sense of purpose.

I am a warrior of love and compassion with my Patka.

The Patka reminds me of my
inner wisdom.

I am grounded and centered with my Patka.

The Patka shields me from
negativity.

Wearing my Patka helps me stay focused.

I am a source of inspiration with my Patka.

I am grateful for the strength that
my Patka gives me.

Wearing my Patka encourages self-care.

I trust the guidance that my Patka
teaches me.

My Patka reminds me of my worth.

My Patka empowers creativity.

Wearing my Patka fosters peace
within me.

I am courageous in the face of
challenges when I wear my Patka.

My Patka aligns me with my
higher purpose.

My Patka connects me with my
inner guidance.

I am a symbol of transformation
with my Patka.

My Patka enhances my self-belief.

Wearing my Patka helps me face
my fears.

My Patka fills me with strength
and love.

When I wear my Patka, I am filled with a profound sense of inner peace and purpose.

I am grateful for the spiritual
strength my Patka gives me.

My Patka is a symbol of my
identity and heritage.

My Patka reminds me to live with
love and compassion.

My Patka represents my
commitment to service.

Wearing my Patka fills me with a
sense of unity.

My Patka empowers me to stand
up for what is right.

Wearing my Patka encourages me
to be selfless.

I trust the guidance of Waheguru
(God) when I wear my Patka.

My Patka reminds me of the
importance of humility.

I am a source of inspiration to others when I wear my Patka.

My Patka enhances my
commitment to truth and honesty.

I am grateful for the wisdom and teachings of the Sikh Gurus when I wear my Patka.

Wearing my Patka encourages me
to lead by example.

My Patka empowers me to practice self-discipline.

I am proud to wear my Patka as it
is an expression of my faith.

Wearing my Patka encourages
me to be kind, just, and
compassionate.

I embrace the power and
protection of my Patka.

Printed in Great Britain
by Amazon